Inspirational
Sermon Outlines

Inspirational Sermon Outlines

Russell E. Spray

BAKER BOOK HOUSE
Grand Rapids, Michigan 49516

Copyright 1988 by Baker Book House Company

ISBN: 0-8010-8288-9

Printed in the United States of America

Contents

Foreword   7

1. "All for Jesus"   8
   Colossians 3:1
2. "A More Excellent N-A-M-E"   10
   Hebrews 1:4
3. "An Understanding Heart"   12
   1 Kings 3:9
4. Be More Like Christ   14
   Acts 4:13
5. Christians Are Different   16
   2 Corinthians 5:17
6. Claim the Promises   18
   Psalm 27:14
7. Dynamics of Faith   20
   Hebrews 11:1
8. Describing the Christian's L-I-G-H-T   22
   Matthew 5:14
9. Facts About Faith   24
   Hebrews 12:2
10. "Have Faith in God"   26
    Mark 11:22
11. How Christians Should G-I-V-E   28
    Acts 20:35
12. How Christians Should W-A-I-T   30
    Psalm 27:14
13. How to Glorify the Lord   32
    Psalm 86:12
14. Let Your Faith G-R-O-W   34
    2 Thessalonians 1:3

15. L-I-V-E More Abundantly 36
    John 10:10
16. P-R-A-I-S-E Is 38
    Psalm 33:1
17. Simplicity of the Gospel 40
    Romans 10:13
18. Successful Christians Are . . . 42
    Isaiah 48:15
19. The C-O-M-F-O-R-T of God 44
    2 Corinthians 1:3-4
20. The Christian's Conquest 46
    1 Corinthians 15:57
21. The Lord H-O-L-D-S His Own 48
    Isaiah 41:13
22. The Power of Praise 50
    Psalm 145:3
23. The Way to Heaven 52
    Isaiah 35:8
24. T-O-T-A-L Surrender 54
    Romans 12:1
25. "These Three" 56
    1 Corinthians 13:13
26. Victorious Living 58
    1 Corinthians 15:57
27. "W-A-I-T on the Lord" 60
    Psalm 27:14

Foreword

Christ is all, and in all (Col. 3:11).

I trust that *Inspirational Sermon Outlines* will encourage Christians to go deeper in Christ and cause sinners to find him.

May these outlines be a blessing to all who use and hear them, I pray. I also pray that God may be glorified.

Russell E. Spray

1

"All for Jesus"

If ye then be risen with Christ, seek those things which are above, where Christ sitteth on the right hand of God (Col. 3:1).

Christians need to fully understand what being "all for Jesus" means. The following points should make it clearer.

I. Living in Jesus
All for Jesus! all for Jesus!
All my being's ransomed pow'rs!:
All my tho'ts and words and doings,
All my days and all my hours.
(First verse of the hymn, "All for Jesus")
   A. "Therefore if any man be in Christ, he is a new creature: old things are passed away; behold, all things are become new" (2 Cor. 5:17).
   B. When we live in Christ, he lives in us also. He controls our life. We are his stewards—of our time, talents and wealth.

II. Lifting Up Jesus
Let my hands perform his bidding;
Let my feet run in his ways;
Let my eyes see Jesus only;
Let my lips speak forth His praise.
(Second verse of the hymn, "All for Jesus")
   A. Jesus said, "And I, if I be lifted up from the earth, will draw all men unto me" (John 12:32).
   B. We help lift up Jesus when we assist the less fortunate, comfort the bereaved and lonely, and witness to the lost about his plan of salvation.

III. Looking to Jesus
Since my eyes were fixed on Jesus,
I've lost sight of all beside,

So enchained my spirit's vision,
Looking at the Crucified.
(Third verse of the hymn, "All for Jesus")

A. "Looking unto Jesus the author and finisher of our faith; who for the joy that was set before him endured the cross . . ." (Heb. 12:2).
B. Many people look to pleasure, popularity, possessions, and other people for their security. We must look to an unfailing Jesus.

IV. Leaning on Jesus

Oh, what wonder! how amazing!
Jesus, glorious King of Kings,
Deigns to call me His beloved.
Lets me rest beneath His wings."
(Fourth verse of the hymn, "All for Jesus")

A. Rest in the LORD, and wait patiently for him (Ps. 37:7). We must lean on the Lord trustingly, depending on him implicitly.
B. "Trust in the LORD with all thine heart; and lean not unto thine own understanding" (Prov. 3:5). "All for Jesus" means living in Jesus, lifting up Jesus, looking to Jesus, and leaning on Jesus at all times.

2

"A More Excellent N-A-M-E"

Being made so much better than the angels, as he hath by inheritance obtained a more excellent name than they (Heb. 1:4).

The scriptures magnify the name of Jesus. We also should magnify the greatness of his N-A-M-E.

I. N-oteworthy Name
Far above all principality, and power, and might, and dominion, and every name that is named . . . (Eph. 1:21).
  A. When Jesus was here on earth, he healed the sick, comforted the sorrowful, forgave the sinful, and there went out a fame of him through all the region round about (Luke 4:14).
  B. The power of Jesus is the same today for those who believe. He saves, sanctifies, satisfies, and sustains when we ask in his name (John 14:13–14). He is worthy of our praise.

II. A-ffectionate Name
. . . thou shalt call his name JESUS: for he shall save his people from their sins (Matt. 1:21).
  A. Love is willing to sacrifice for the object of its affection. Many Christians are lacking in love because they fail to deny themselves for God and others.
  B. Jesus willingly died on the cross for our sins because he loved us so much (John 10:18). When we comfort, pray, and care for others in Jesus' name, we increase in love and glorify the Lord (John 15:9–12).

III. M-ajestic Name
A name which is above every name: That at the name of Jesus every knee should bow . . . (Phil. 2:9–10).
  A. Many Christians are concerned with exalting themselves and obtaining recognition, but are lax about honoring the name of Jesus.

B. Majestic means—"very grand or dignified; lofty; stately . . ."—Webster. The name of Jesus defies definition. It is above every name (Phil. 2:9). If he is the King of kings and Lord of lords in our life, we should praise and exalt him more.

IV. E-verlasting Name

His name shall be called . . . The everlasting Father . . ." (Isa. 9:6).

A. Few things in our world are lasting. Possessions are temporal; they wear out, rust and decay.
B. Only those who accept the Lord have something of everlasting value—eternity with God in heaven. "And they shall see his face; and his name shall be in their foreheads" (Rev. 22:4).

3

"An Understanding Heart"

Give therefore thy servant an understanding heart . . . that I may discern between good and bad (1 Kings 3:9).

An understanding heart pleases God and helps Christians accomplish his work on earth more effectively.

I. Cares
Casting all your care upon him; for he careth for you (1 Peter 5:7).
  A. Millions of people do not care enough about others. They are selfishly motivated, and seek their own welfare and profit.
  B. God cared so much he gave his only begotten son to die on the cross for us (John 3:16).
  C. We must care about others. Understanding hearts are concerned when others are in need and hurting.

II. Dares
Who gave himself a ransom for all . . . (1 Tim. 2:6).
  A. Many people fail to get involved in the difficulties of others. Doing so would interfere with their own concerns.
  B. When mankind was lost and without hope, Christ became involved. He gave his life to atone for our sins.
  C. Christian love dares to get involved; it reaches out to help those who are in trouble (2 Cor. 1:4).

III. Spares
He that loseth his life for my sake shall find it (Matt. 10:39).
  A. Many seek to spare themselves misfortune and loss even at the expense of others.
  B. Jesus did not spare himself, but to the contrary, he gave himself to spare others. He took our place on the cross, paying the penalty for our sins (Rom. 8:32).

C. An understanding heart seeks to spare others. We must be willing to suffer loss as unto the Lord.

IV. Shares

Give, and it shall be given unto you (Luke 6:38).

A. Some are ready to receive a smile, a kind word, or a good deed, but they are reluctant to give to others.
B. Christ gave himself that we might enjoy salvation now and share heaven with him in the life to come (John 14:1–3).
C. We must share our moments, money, and skills also. An understanding heart cares, dares, spares, and shares.

4

Be More Like Christ

And they took knowledge of them, that they had been with Jesus (Acts 4:13).

Let the following points serve as a guide in our endeavor to be more like Jesus.

I. Think as Christ Did
Let this mind be in you, which was also in Christ Jesus (Phil. 2:5).
- A. Jesus told his disciples, "If ye have faith as a grain of mustard seed, ye shall say unto this mountain, Remove hence to yonder place; and it shall remove" (Matt. 17:20).
- B. We need positive faith. Negative thoughts must be replaced with positive ones.

II. See as Christ Did
But when he saw the multitudes, he was moved with compassion on them . . . (Matt. 9:36).
- A. Jesus looked with compassion on the sick, suffering, and sinful. He is touched with the feeling of our infirmities (Heb. 4:15).
- B. We also should be moved with compassion toward those in need and help those who carry burdens.

III. Hear as Christ Did
The righteous cry, and the Lord heareth, and delivereth them out of all their troubles (Ps. 34:17).
- A. Christ was never too busy to hear the cry of his people. He hears our petitions when we cry unto him.
- B. We too should be ready to listen to those who are troubled and lonely.

IV. Talk as Christ Did
[All] wondered at the gracious words which proceeded out of his mouth (Luke 4:22).
- A. Christ brought salvation down to mankind. He talked about faith, hope, love, joy, and peace.
- B. We should talk about spiritual matters also, to be more concerned with eternal than materialistic values.

V. Do as Christ Did
I must work the works of him that sent me, while it is day: the night cometh, when no man can work (John 9:4).
- A. Christ did the work his Heavenly Father sent him to do (Luke 4:18).
- B. Many Christians are overly interested in their own concerns. They scarcely have time left to do God's work.

VI. Go as Christ Did
Who went about doing good . . . (Acts 10:38).
- A. We must be on the go for God, helping the grieving, suffering, and those who do not know Christ.
- B. Christ, our example, was on the go, seeking to help the needy and save the lost. If we go for God, he will go for us.

5

Christians Are Different

If any man be in Christ, he is a new creature: old things are passed away; behold all things are become new (2 Cor. 5:17).

Christians are different from the world. They have been made new, therefore they are—

I. Changed by Christ
   A. Christians have repented of their sins and are forgiven.
   B. Christians have new ambitions and goals. Their heart, desires, and hopes have been changed. They now seek to please God (1 John 2:5).

II. Committed to Christ
I know whom I have believed, and am persuaded that he is able to keep that which I have committed unto him . . . (2 Tim. 1:12).
   A. Many people insist on going their own way and doing what they choose. They falter and fail spiritually.
   B. Totally surrendered Christians are committed to Christ. They yield unreservedly to his way and will. They are cleansed by faith and filled with the Holy Spirit (Acts 15:8–9).

III. Confident in Christ
I can do all things through Christ which strengtheneth me (Phil. 4:13).
   A. The apostle Paul was confident in Christ. He was aware of his own weaknesses but sure of God's indwelling power.
   B. We must be confident in Christ also, claiming his promise of grace and strength as Paul did (2 Cor. 12:9).

IV. Courageous for Christ
With all boldness as always, so now also Christ shall be magnified in my body whether it be by life, or by death (Phil. 1:20).

A. Paul was ready to put his life on the line for Christ. He was yielded to him without reserve.
B. Today completely dedicated Christians are courageous for Christ too. We must give him first place in our life. "Seek ye first the kingdom of God" (Matt. 6:33).

V. (Will Be) Caught Up with Christ

We which are alive and remain shall be caught up together with them in the clouds, to meet the Lord in the air (1 Thess. 4:17).

A. For centuries Christians have been looking for the coming of the Lord. His coming must be soon (1 Thess. 5:2).
B. Those who are changed by Christ, committed to Christ, confident in Christ, and courageous for Christ shall be caught up with Him. "And so shall we ever be with the Lord" (1 Thess. 4:17).

6

Claim the Promise

Wait on the LORD: be of good courage, and he shall strengthen thine heart: wait, I say, on the LORD (Ps. 27:14).

Waiting isn't easy, but those who learn to wait on the Lord shall receive his promised strength. Therefore—

I. Be Patient
Wait on the LORD (Ps. 27:14).
   A. Many Christians lack patience. They expect God's will to agree with their will instead of aligning their will with his, to receive his blessings in their appointed time.
   B. To claim the promise and receive God's blessings, we must wait God's time. His timing is always best, and it is never too late (Ps. 37:7–9).

II. Be Positive
Be of good courage . . . (Ps. 27:14).
   A. Christians are often a poor witness because of their negative approach to life. Their tones and gestures give them away, negating their good intentions.
   B. We must practice praising God and being thankful. To claim the promise, we must look for the good and reach for the best (Ps. 35:27–28).

III. Be Powerful
And he shall strengthen thine heart (Ps. 27:14).
   A. Christians are admonished to be strong in the Lord, and in the power of his might (Eph. 6:10).
   B. Paul declared, "I can do all things through Christ which strengtheneth me" (Phil. 4:13). God gives inner strength to his trusting children.

IV. Be Persevering
Wait, I say, on the LORD (Ps. 27:14).
- A. Many Christians give up too easily. When adverse conditions come, they throw up their hands in despair. We must keep on keeping on.
- B. We must never give up, no matter how difficult the circumstances. A crown of righteousness awaits those who keep on working for and waiting on the Lord (2 Tim. 4:8).

7

Dynamics of Faith

Now faith is the substance of things hoped for, the evidence of things not seen (Heb. 11:1).

Without faith it is impossible to please God. Therefore, let us consider the—

I. Who of Faith
Have faith in God (Mark 11:22).
- A. Many people put their faith in other people, possessions, real estate, stocks and bonds, etc. They often come to disappointment (1 Tim. 6:10).
- B. Our faith must be placed in God. Friends, loved ones, personal gain may fail, but Jesus never fails (Heb. 12:2).

II. What of Faith
All things, whatsoever ye shall ask in prayer, believing, ye shall receive (Matt. 21:22).
- A. Many Christians depend solely on finite strength. It fails. Nothing is too difficult for God's infinite power. He can do "all things."
- B. We must exert our efforts while believing God is working through us. Our faith and God's power make "all things" possible (Mark 9:23).

III. Where of Faith
I will therefore that men pray every where, lifting up holy hands, without wrath and doubting (1 Tim. 2:8).
- A. Some places lend themselves more readily to an attitude of prayer and faith. But we must pray everywhere—at home, school, work, and play.
- B. Walking among the throngs of a large city or driving down a busy street—wherever we are, we can be in a spirit of believ-

ing prayer. By faith Abraham . . . obeyed; and he went out (Heb. 11:8). We can go for God by faith too.

IV. When of Faith

When ye pray, believe that ye receive them, and ye shall have them (Mark 11:24).

A. Many Christians want to receive first and then believe. To be effective we must believe first.
B. The "who" of faith is God; the "what" refers to everything; the "where" pertains to all places; the "when" means now and always; and, the "why" of faith has to do with pleasing him.

V. Why of Faith

Without faith it is impossible to please him (Heb. 11:6).

A. God gave each of us a "measure of faith" (Rom. 12:3) and ordained that "the just shall live by faith" (Gal. 3:11). Faith increases as we use what we have.
B. Faith pleases God and brings his blessings. We receive God through faith and we receive from God through faith. Faith is of utmost importance.

8

Describing the Christian's L-I-G-H-T

Ye are the light of the world. A city that is set on an hill cannot be hid (Matt. 5:14).

Christians should let their light shine. L-I-G-H-T should be—

I. L-uminous
Luminous means "giving off light; shining; bright . . . glowing in the dark"—Webster.
  A. Many Christians fail to let their light shine for God. Some are self-conscious; others too occupied with personal pursuits.
  B. We must take time for God. The world is groping in sin's darkness. Perhaps a smile, a cheery word, or a warm handshake will be a blessing to one in despair (Matt. 5:16).

II. I-nviting
Among whom ye shine as lights in the world; Holding forth the word of life (Phil. 2:15–16).
  A. In today's world many are cold, indifferent, and unfriendly. They lack the warmth of the Holy Spirit and God's love.
  B. Millions are searching for care and understanding. The Christian's light should be attractive. Inviting. (Prov. 4:18).

III. G-enuine
Genuine means "not counterfeit or artificial; real; true; authentic . . . sincere and frank; honest and forthright"—Webster.
  A. Most of the glittering, dazzling attractions in our world are deceiving (2 Cor. 11:14). They undermine and destroy moral and spiritual values.
  B. Christ is the light of the world (John 1:9). We must let his light shine through us to bless others.

IV. H-elpful

Let your light so shine before men, that they may see your good works, and glorify your Father which is in heaven (Matt. 5:16).

A. Many are lost in the night of sin and need guidance and direction. The Christian's light should serve as a beacon.
B. We can let our light shine by lending a helping hand to the needy, and comforting the bereaved and lonely (Luke 12:35).

V. T-imeless

Timeless means "that cannot be measured by time; unending . . . transcending time; eternal"—Webster.

A. The light of the selfishly motivated soon goes out. God's promise to his trusting children is this: The LORD shall be unto thee an everlasting light and thy God thy glory (Isa. 60:19).
B. The Christian's light should be luminous, inviting, genuine, and helpful. If so, his light shall continue to shine forever, for the light of Christ shall illuminate his pathway through this world to the land to come (Rev. 21:23).

9

Facts About Faith

Looking unto Jesus the author and finisher of our faith; who . . . endured the cross, despising the shame, and is set down at the right hand of the throne of God (Heb. 12:2).

The following facts about faith should offer insight into the value and working of faith in the lives of Christians. Consider—

I. Its Truth
Now faith is the substance of things hoped for, the evidence of things not seen (Heb. 11:1).
- A. The Word of God declares Jesus Christ to be the "truth." He is the author and finisher of our faith (Heb. 12:2).
- B. For centuries faith in Christ has been tested and found to be true. The reality of faith is evidenced throughout the Bible.
- C. Salvation through Christ is received by faith. ". . . that whosoever believeth in him should not perish but have everlasting life" (John 3:16).

II. Its Trial
That the trial of your faith . . . might be found unto praise and glory at the appearing of Jesus Christ (1 Peter 1:7).
- A. Because the Christian's faith is valuable, God sometimes allows it to be tested "as by fire."
- B. Trials should strengthen and refine our faith. They often teach us lessons, training us for God's service.
- C. We must accept what God allows, using it to his glory. "God is faithful, who will not suffer you to be tempted above that ye are able . . ." (1 Cor. 10:13).

III. Its Touch
But Jesus . . . said . . . thy faith hath made thee whole (Matt. 9:22).

- A. Jesus healed this woman because of her faith. For she said, "If I may touch his garment, I shall be whole" (Matt. 9:21).
- B. The touch of Christ through faith is needed by all Christians not only at special times but daily.
- C. We must submit to God's method. He often uses medical science and our faith to heal physically, mentally, and spiritually.

IV. Its Triumph

I have kept the faith: Henceforth there is laid up for me a crown of righteousness . . . (2 Tim. 4:7–8).

- A. On the eve of Paul's departure, he declared, "I have fought a good fight, I have finished my course, I have kept the faith . . ."
- B. We must likewise keep the faith. Through bad as well as good times, through difficulties as well as times of ease, we can triumph in the faith.
- C. The truth, trial, touch, and triumph of faith increase present faith and assure us of eternal life to come.

10

Have Faith in God

And Jesus answering saith unto them, Have faith in God (Mark 11:22).

In Mark 11:23–24 Jesus talked about the possibilities that are ours through faith. We must "have faith in God."

I. **Have—**
   According as God hath dealt to every man the measure of faith (Rom. 12:3).
   A. God gives each of us a "measure of faith." However, we must cooperate with him if we are to develop and increase our faith, for we are labourers together with God (1 Cor. 3:9).
   B. Accomplishment requires effort. When we work our faith, our faith works for us. We must have faith to *do for* God as well as *to receive from* God.

II. **Faith—**
   Faith is the substance of things hoped for, the evidence of things not seen (Heb. 11:1).
   A. The value of faith cannot be estimated. We are saved by faith, sanctified by faith, and sustained by faith. Without faith it is impossible to please him (Heb. 11:6).
   B. When the father of the afflicted boy asked Jesus to heal his son, Jesus said, "All things are possible to him that believeth" (Mark 9:23).

III. **In—**
   Nor trust in uncertain riches, but in the living God . . . (1 Tim. 6:17).
   A. When the disciples' ship was tossed about by the winds and waves, Jesus calmed the storm. Then he asked, "Where is your faith?" (Luke 8:25).
   B. To "have faith" our trust must be "in" something or some-

one. Is your faith in houses and lands, silver and gold, pleasure or position, or in other people? Where is your faith?

IV. God—

Have faith in God (Mark 11:22).

A. Our faith must be in God. He is our strength, safety, and security. We must recognize his greatness, goodness, and graciousness (1 Peter 2:3).

B. Prayer, the promises, promoting God's work, and praising him increase our faith. Let us begin now. "Have faith in God" (Mark 11:22).

11

How Christians Should G-I-V-E

It is more blessed to give than to receive (Acts 20:35).

It is important for Christians to be generous. The following points assist us in knowing how we should G-I-V-E.

I. G-enerously
Give, and it shall be given unto you; good measure, pressed down, and shaken together, and running over . . . (Luke 6:38).
- A. When it comes to giving for God, many Christians fall short. They give as little as possible, unless selfish reasons are involved.
- B. We must give liberally and as unto the Lord. We never can outgive God. "If it is contributing to the needs of others, let him give generously" (Rom. 12:8, NIV).

II. I-nconspicuously
Let not thy left hand know what thy right hand doeth (Matt. 6:3).
- A. When Jesus was here on earth, He condemned the hypocrites who gave to impress others and draw attention to themselves that they may have glory of men. He said, "They have their reward" (Matt. 6:2).
- B. Christians should give of their means to glorify God and be a blessing to others. God will reward the faithful in his own time and way.

III. V-oluntarily
According as he purposeth in his heart, so let him give; not grudgingly, or of necessity . . . (2 Cor. 9:7).
- A. Some Christians are spasmodic in their giving. They give when they feel like giving. Our commitment to God should include our resources as well as our time and abilities.
- B. If we are to help build God's Kingdom, we must give

willingly and consistently, not grudgingly, or of necessity . . . (2 Cor. 9:7).

IV. E-njoyably

For God loveth a cheerful giver (2 Cor. 9:7).

A. Perhaps some do not receive a blessing from giving because they do not give joyfully. Joyful giving pleases God and brings his approbation.
B. Christians should give generously, inconspicuously, voluntarily and enjoyably. As Jesus said, "It is more blessed to give than to receive" (Acts 20:35).

12

How Christians Should Wait

Wait on the LORD: be of good courage, and he shall strengthen thine heart: wait, I say, on the LORD (Ps. 27:14).

Waiting can be difficult. The following points tell us how we should wait.

I. Wait with Prayer
Pray without ceasing (1 Thess. 5:17).
  A. In times that require waiting, Christians should be much in prayer. They should bring everything to God and claim his promises.
  B. We should continue in a spirit of prayer in busy times as well. "Praying always with all prayer and supplication in the Spirit" . . . (Eph. 6:18).

II. Wait with Patience
In your patience possess ye your souls (Luke 21:19).
  A. People wait in line at the grocery store. They wait at the doctor's office and many other places, but they often wait impatiently.
  B. Patience makes the Christian's testimony more effective. Waiting may be a difficult thing to do, but we should practice doing it with patience (James 1:4).

III. Wait with Purpose
That with purpose of heart they would cleave unto the Lord (Acts 11:23).
  A. Christ came to earth with a purpose. He came to die for our sins and to glorify his Heavenly Father.
  B. God has a purpose for his earthly children also. Each should seek God's individualized will for his life and then be occupied doing God's work while he waits. "Having made known unto us the mystery of his will . . ." (Eph. 1:9).

IV. Wait with Praise

I will bless the LORD at all times: his praise shall continually be in my mouth (Ps. 34:1).

  A. Many fail to praise the Lord as they should. They complain or even blame God for their difficulties.
  B. The Lord is worthy of all our praise. We should offer our thanks and praise in bad as well as good times. "In every thing give thanks" (1 Thess. 5:18).

13

How to Glorify the Lord

I will praise thee, O LORD my God, with all my heart: and I will glorify thy name for evermore (Ps. 86:12).

Many fail to glorify the Lord as they should. Let us investigate some of the ways to do so.

I. Live in the Lord
If any man be in Christ, he is a new creature (2 Cor. 5:17).
- A. To live in Christ, we must be "in Christ"—having repented of our sins, believed on Christ, and accepted him as our personal Savior.
- B. Christ is our example. We must follow in his steps. We must walk uprightly, guarding our words, thoughts, and deeds.
- C. Let us live so others will want to follow Christ also. We glorify the Lord by doing those things that please him (1 Thess. 4:1).

II. Lean on the Lord
Casting all your care upon him; for he careth for you (1 Peter 5:7).
- A. Many Christians fail to completely lean on the Lord. They rely on other people—doctors, lawyers, or friends.
- B. We cannot meet life's demands in our own strength or the strength of others. Only the help of the Lord will suffice.
- C. We should trust in the Lord with all our heart and lean not unto our own understanding (Prov. 3:5).

III. Lift with the Lord
For we are labourers together with God . . . (1 Cor. 3:9).
- A. Many Christians are remiss when it comes to doing God's work. They are too busily engaged in personal pursuits.
- B. We are not independently doing God's work. We are workers

together with the Lord. He will help us as we give him first place (Matt. 6:33).
C. We glorify the Lord when we give a smile, say a kind word, or do a good deed for a needy person.

IV. Look for the Lord

Looking for that blessed hope, and the glorious appearing of . . . Jesus Christ (Titus 2:13).

A. Many Christians are not expecting the Lord's soon return. They are too involved with possessions, popularity, and promotions.
B. We glorify the Lord as we continually watch for his return. We must not become slack concerning his promise to reappear.
C. The scripture reminds us, "For the Lord himself shall descend from heaven with a shout . . . and so shall we ever be with the Lord" (1 Thess. 4:16–17). Read 1 Thess. 4:15–18.

14

Let Your Faith G-R-O-W

Your faith groweth exceedingly, and the charity of every one of you all toward each other aboundeth (2 Thess. 1:3).

The faith of Christians should not stagnate. It should continue to grow. To G-R-O-W in faith means to please God.

I. G-reat Faith
O woman, great is thy faith (Matt. 15:28).
   A. When Jesus was here on earth, he admired and honored persevering faith. "And her daughter was made whole from that very hour."
   B. Jesus was displeased when his disciples were weak in faith. He said, "O ye of little faith . . ." (Matt. 8:26). The Lord will help us develop great faith through prayer and perseverance.

II. R-eliable Faith
I have kept the faith (2 Tim. 4:7).
   A. The apostle Paul experienced hardship during his lifetime, but when he came to the end of his life, he was able to declare, "I have kept the faith."
   B. We can keep the faith also if we keep on day by day despite frustration, failure, and persecution. Like Paul, we can be assured of receiving a crown of righteousness at the end of our earthly journey (2 Tim. 4:8).

III. O-bedient Faith
By faith Abraham . . . obeyed . . . (Heb. 11:8).
   A. Abraham depended on God for direction. By faith he sojourned in the land of promise, as in a strange country . . . (Heb. 11:9).
   B. We must have obedient faith too. God's promise to those who follow his instructions is, "I will guide thee with mine eye" (Ps. 32:8).

IV. W-orking Faith

Even so faith, if it hath not works, is dead, being alone (James 2:17).

A. Many Christians are remiss when it comes to doing God's work. Their faith dwindles because they fail to use and exercise it.
B. To have a growing faith, we must have a working faith. Christians must be ready to help the needy, comfort the lonely, and share Christ with the unsaved (Col. 3:12–14).

15

L-I-V-E More Abundantly

I am come that they might have life, and that they might have it more abundantly (John 10:10).

Christians need to do the following things in order to L-I-V-E more abundantly.

I. L-ove God and Others
By this we know that we love the children of God, when we love God, and keep his commandments (1 John 5:12).
  A. Many declare they love God but fail to pray for others. They lack concern, compassion, and a caring heart.
  B. To truly love God means loving others also. "And this commandment have we from him, That he that loveth God love his brother also" (1 John 4:21).

II. I-nvest in God's Kingdom
Seek ye first the kingdom of God, and his righteousness . . . (Matt. 6:33).
  A. In today's affluent society, millions of people are investing in temporal pursuits. Too many have set their heart on making money and gaining possessions.
  B. We must faithfully give of ourselves and our assets. "Set your affection on things above, not on things on the earth" (Col. 3:2).

III. V-olunteer for God's Service
That thy benefit should not be as it were of necessity, but willingly (Philem. 14).
  A. Some Christians seldom offer to do God's service. They wait to be drafted. Willing workers live more abundantly.
  B. We must be ready to do God's work willingly and heartily as unto the Lord, enduring hardness, as a good soldier of Jesus Christ (2 Tim. 2:3).

IV. E-ndure to the End

He that shall endure unto the end, the same shall be saved (Matt. 24:13).

  A. Many fail to live abundant lives because they give up too easily. When adversities assail, they throw up their hands in despair.
  B. Christians need not be defeated. They can endure through Christ. "Nay, in all these things, we are more than conquerors through him who loved us" (Rom. 8:37).

16

P-R-A-I-S-E Is . . .

Rejoice in the LORD, O ye righteous: for praise is comely for the upright (Ps. 33:1).

Christians should praise the Lord more. We can praise him in the following ways. P-R-A-I-S-E is—

I. P-raying
With thanksgiving let your requests be made known unto God (Phil. 4:6).
   A. Praising the Lord is a must if Christians are to be effective in their prayer life.
   B. God is pleased when we bring our petitions to him with praise.

II. R-ejoicing
But let the righteous . . . rejoice before God . . . sing praises to his name (Ps. 68:3–4).
   A. Many Christians lack joy because they fail to praise the Lord more.
   B. Rejoice in his salvation by deliberately praising God in bad times as well as in happy ones (Ps. 9:14).

III. A-ccepting
I delight to do thy will, O my God (Ps. 40:8).
   A. We must accept both the bitter and the sweet. God works them together for our good and his glory (Rom. 8:28).
   B. Praise is accepting God's will unreservedly (Matt. 6:10).

IV. I-nvesting
Lay not up for yourselves treasures upon earth . . . but lay up for yourselves treasures in heaven (Matt. 6:19–20).
   A. Millions come to disappointment because they invest all their efforts in pursuing earthly interests.

B. If we promote God's kingdom here on earth, we shall rejoice with eternal treasure in the life to come (Ps. 103:2).

V. S-erving
Fervent in spirit; serving the Lord (Rom. 12:11).
- A. Many Christians praise the Lord verbally but are remiss when it comes to serving in his vineyard.
- B. We must praise the Lord not only with our thoughts and words, but also with our deeds and actions.

VI. E-verlasting
So we thy people . . . will give thee thanks forever: we shall shew forth thy praise to all generations (Ps. 79:13).
- A. God has done so much for us that we can never praise him adequately.
- B. Praise is praying, rejoicing, accepting, investing, and serving here on earth. Praise is also nonending, for we shall praise God throughout eternity (Ps. 145:2).

17

Simplicity of the Gospel

For whosoever shall call upon the name of the Lord shall be saved (Rom. 10:13).

No doubt many fail to accept the gospel because they fear it is too difficult to understand. The following outline explains the simplicity of the gospel.

I. The People
For whosoever . . .
- A. We live in a complex society. Requirements for belonging to certain cliques are many—sexual discrimination, age, race, religion, educational attainments, and social standing are involved.
- B. In our society partiality is often shown because of one's political views, popularity, or the attainment of possessions.
- C. The gospel of Jesus Christ is for everybody. It is without partiality and discrimination. The rich and poor, great and small, and young and old alike may receive it (John 3:16).

II. The Petition
. . . shall call upon the name of the Lord . . .
- A. Millions of people are calling on others for help. They depend on doctors, lawyers, loved ones, and friends for their needs.
- B. Because of today's busy and overpopulated society, many calls go unheeded. Tragedy and death often occur because of neglect and unconcern.
- C. The Lord cares about our deepest needs. He is ready to help those who call upon him in humility and faith. Bring your petitions to the Lord. He is never too busy (Ps. 20:5).

III. The Promise
   . . . shall be saved.
   A. Many Christians fail to keep promises as they should. Politicians galore have promised better living conditions and social justice, only to bring disappointment to the masses.
   B. God's promises never fail. He is the only one who can forgive sins and satisfy the longing of the soul. He has promised to do so (Ps. 107:9).
   C. We must confess our sins and commit our life to God in simple, trusting faith. "He is faithful and just to forgive us our sins, and to cleanse us from all unrighteousness" (1 John 1:9).

18
Successful Christians Are . . .

I, even I, have spoken; yea, I have called him: I have brought him, and he shall make his way prosperous (Isa. 48:15).

We need not fail in our spiritual life. We can be victorious and influential. Successful Christians are—

I. Growing Christians
May grow up into him in all things . . . (Eph. 4:15).
- A. Many Christians are living defeated lives because they fail to grow spiritually as they should. God wants us to "grow up" (mature) into him in all things.
- B. Successful Christians continually progress. Their spiritual growth may slow down at times, but it should continue to grow even during periods of difficulty.
- C. Spiritual growth comes through prayer, praise, meditation on God's Word, and the performance of the tasks he gives us to do. (2 Peter 3:18).

II. Glowing Christians
Let your light so shine before men, that they may see your good works, and glorify your Father which is in heaven (Matt. 5:16).
- A. Too many Christians fail to let their light shine. They are too busy receiving honor for themselves rather than seeking to glorify God.
- B. Some are hindered by inferiority feelings. Many are too occupied pursuing personal gain.
- C. Christians must let their light shine. Their testimony can be a blessing to other Christians. It can also serve as a beacon to guide the lost into the harbor of safety (Matt. 5:14–15).

III. Going Christians
I have chosen you . . . that ye should go and bring forth fruit . . . (John 15:16).
- A. Many Christians lack enthusiasm for God's Kingdom here on earth. They fail to "go and bring forth fruit" for God.
- B. Successful Christians are going Christians. They readily assist the less fortunate, visit the sick and lonely, and share Christ with the unsaved.
- C. When Christians go for God, he goes with them. We are not alone in our efforts. "For we are labourers together with God" (1 Cor. 3:9).

19

The C-O-M-F-O-R-T of God

Blessed be . . . the God of all comfort; who comforteth us in all our tribulation, that we may be able to comfort them which are in any trouble (2 Cor. 1:3–4).

This acrostical outline points out ways that God uses to comfort his trusting children.

I. C-aring Comfort
For he careth for you (1 Peter 5:7).
A. It is comforting to know that God cares for his own.
B. We must also comfort others, care for them, be mindful of their needs (2 Cor. 1:4).

II. O-mnipresent Comfort
I will never leave thee, nor forsake thee (Heb. 13:5).
A. Realizing God is with us at all times brings great comfort.
B. We may not always feel God's presence because of circumstances, but he is present anyway (Isa. 41:10).

III. M-erciful Comfort
The Lord is very pitiful, and of tender mercy (James 5:11).
A. God's mercy extends to the uttermost parts of the earth. It comforts and endures.
B. We must be merciful, comforting those who seem undeserving (Col. 3:12).

IV. F-ortifying Comfort
He is my refuge and my fortress (Ps. 91:2).
A. The psalmist placed his trust in God and received his fortifying comfort.
B. We must depend on God to fortify us during times of adversity also. "In him will I trust" (Ps. 91:2).

V. O-vercoming Comfort
Be of good cheer; I have overcome the world (John 16:33).
- A. Because Jesus overcame the world, we can overcome also.
- B. The power of Christ is infinite and neverfailing. We can overcome only through the strength he gives (Phil. 4:13).

VI. R-eassuring Comfort
He shall call upon me, and I will answer him (Ps. 91:15).
- A. When the psalmist cried unto the Lord, he was reassured of divine help.
- B. When we pray and believe God's promises, we are strengthened and sustained through Christ. The promises of his strength bring reassurance to us (Isa. 40:31).

VII. T-rustworthy Comfort
For I am the LORD, I change not (Mal. 3:6).
- A. It is comforting to know that the Lord is dependable and unchanging in an undependable and ever-changing world.
- B. Jesus Christ is the same yesterday, and today, and for ever (Heb. 13:8). As we depend on him, let us be trustworthy when it comes to comforting others—"by the comfort wherewith we ourselves are comforted of God" (2 Cor. 1:4).

20

The Christian's Conquest

But thanks be to God, which giveth us the victory through our Lord Jesus Christ (1 Cor. 15:57).

Christians can be victorious over Satan. They can glorify God and be a blessing to others. The following points show us how:

I. The Praise
But thanks be to God.
- A. Some Christians fail to praise the Lord enough. Perhaps they praise him when everything is going their way but refrain when times get tough.
- B. We should remember that God has a purpose in every thing he allows. He works both the good and the bad together for our good and his glory (Rom. 8:28).
- C. We may not understand the circumstances but we must continue to praise the Lord. We should say with the psalmist, "I will praise thee for ever, because thou hast done it" (Ps. 52:9).

II. The Power
Who giveth us the victory . . .
- A. Many Christians live beneath their privilege. They suffer defeat instead of experiencing victory when tried and tested.
- B. God's grace and power are sufficient for his trusting children. He is more than a match for Satan and we are conquerors through him (Rom. 8:35-36).
- C. God has promised, "When thou passeth through the waters, I will be with thee: and through the rivers, they shall not overflow thee . . ." (Isa. 43:2).

III. The Person
   . . . Through our Lord Jesus Christ.
   A. Mankind lost fellowship with God through disobedience. Jesus Christ is the person who restored our fellowship with God. Through his death on the cross we can be saved.
   B. We cannot save ourselves. We are finite beings. Jesus Christ, the person, is infinite. He brings salvation and strength to those who repent and believe him.
   C. With the apostle Paul we can declare, "I can do all things through Christ who strengtheneth me" (Phil. 4:13). He is *the* person. He never fails.

21

The Lord H-O-L-D-S His Own

For I the LORD thy God will hold thy right hand, saying unto thee, Fear not; I will help thee (Isa. 41:13).

The following points deal with some of the ways the Lord H-O-L-D-S his own:

I. H-elps His Own
I will strengthen thee; yea, I will help thee (Isa. 41:10).
A. Many Christians try to cope with the stresses of life in their own strength. They flounder and fail.
B. We cannot meet the challenges of life in our own power. We need the power of God to help us.

II. O-versees His Own
I will guide thee with mine eye (Ps. 32:8).
A. Many people live alone with no one to watch over them. Those who have the Lord are never alone.
B. The Lord oversees his people. He never slumbers nor sleeps. He sees them at all times (Ps. 121:3–4).

III. L-eads His Own
Even there shall thy hand lead me, and thy right hand shall hold me (Ps. 139:10).
A. The psalmist was assured of God's direction—even in the most extreme circumstances (Ps. 139:8–9).
B. The Lord will guide his people safely through today's dangerous and devastating conditions also.

IV. D-elivers His Own
I have made, and I will bear; even I will carry, and will deliver you (Isa. 46:4).
A. Millions of people need deliverance. They are in bondage to sin, Satan, and self.

B. God has promised to deliver those who trust in him. He brings freedom from selfish motivation, sensual lust, and sinful pride.

V. S-ustains His Own

Cast thy burden upon the Lord, and he shall sustain thee (Ps. 55:22).

A. Many Christians take their burdens to the Lord but fail to leave them there. They fail to relinquish them unconditionally to God.
B. The Lord sustains those who leave their burdens with him. "Casting all your care upon him; for he careth for you" (1 Peter 5:7).

22

The Power of Praise

Great is the LORD, and greatly to be praised; and his greatness is unsearchable (Ps. 145:3).

Christians should be encouraged to praise the Lord more as they consider the who, what, where, when and why of praise.

I. "Who" of Praise
Let the people praise thee, O God; let all the people praise thee (Ps. 67:3).
- A. Many people sing the praises of other humans. Some boast of their own accomplishments rather than praising God.
- B. We should praise God for our blessings, and recognize our abilities come from the good hand of God (Ps. 146:1).

II. "What" of Praise
Giving thanks always for all things unto God . . . (Eph. 5:20).
- A. Many Christians have no difficulty praising God for the good, but they seldom, if ever, praise him for the unpleasant.
- B. We should praise God "for all things," realizing he has a purpose for all he allows to come to his children (1 Thess. 5:18).

III. "Where of Praise
According to thy name, O God, so is thy praise unto the ends of the earth (Ps. 48:10).
- A. Some are ready to praise the Lord when they are on the mountaintop but not in the valley. But praise is an act of faith.
- B. Christians should praise the Lord wherever they are—at home, school, work, play—everywhere.

IV. "When" of Praise

I will bless the LORD at all times; his praise shall continually be in my mouth (Ps. 34:1).

A. Many Christians praise the Lord spasmodically. Some praise him when they feel good and blame him when they feel badly.
B. We should praise "the Lord at all times." Praising God lifts our spirits and changes our outlook. We can never praise the Lord enough (Ps. 145:2).

V. "Why" of Praise

I will praise thee, O LORD my God, with all my heart: and I will glorify thy name for evermore (Ps. 86:12).

A. God is worthy of all our praise; it pleases and glorifies him. Praise to God enables us to receive his blessing and in turn, to be a blessing to others.
B. The "who" of praise is God; the "what" of praise is everything; the "where" of praise is everywhere; the "when" of praise is at all times; and, the "why" of praise is to glorify and honor God (Ps. 145:8–10).

23

The Way to Heaven

And an highway shall be there, and a way, and it shall be called The way of holiness (Isa. 35:8).

Christians want to know more about the way to heaven. It is:

I. A Holy Way
. . . and it shall be called The way of holiness.
  A. Many Christians keep a portion of their life in reserve for selfish pursuits. The Lord commands, "Ye shall be holy: for I the LORD your God am holy" (Lev. 19:2).
  B. To be holy we must surrender our will, way, walk, and wealth to God. We must make a total commitment of ourselves to him, giving God first place in our life (Matt. 6:33).
  C. When we consecrate our all to God, the Holy Spirit cleanses our heart and fills us with God's love and presence. We are on our way to heaven.

II. A Harmless Way
No lion shall be there . . . but the redeemed shall walk there (Isa. 35:9).
  A. Illicit drugs, sex, and terrorism have taken over our society. Ours is a dangerous and destructive world.
  B. The Lord is our hope and safety. He will see us through every difficulty that we must face. "For he shall give his angels charge over thee, to keep thee in all thy ways" (Ps. 91:11).
  C. Our love and trust bring God's protective care. "Because he hath set his love upon me, therefore will I deliver him" (Ps. 91:14).

III. A Happy Way
They shall obtain joy and gladness, and sorrow and sighing shall flee away (Isa. 35:10).

A. All of us seek happiness. We look to houses and lands, silver and gold, and diamonds and pearls, but we fail to find real and lasting joy.
B. We go to doctors, lawyers, or friends trying to find happiness. Still, we are unfulfilled.
C. We must appreciate the help we receive from others but our ultimate trust must be in God. He alone can bring real and lasting peace, joy, and happiness. The way to heaven is a happy way (Ps. 146:5).

24

T-O-T-A-L Surrender

I beseech you therefore, brethren, by the mercies of God, that ye present your bodies a living sacrifice, holy, acceptable unto God, which is your reasonable service (Rom. 12:1).

Christians please God when they give themselves unto Him in T-O-T-A-L surrender.

I. T-urn

To turn them from darkness to light . . . that they may receive forgiveness of sins, and inheritance among them which are sanctified (Acts 26:18).

A. Many people profess to be Christians but have failed to turn completely from their sinful ways to God's ways. They are self-righteous and self-seeking.

B. To turn "from darkness to light" we must repent of our sins and receive God's forgiveness. We must also yield without reserve to God for cleansing.

II. O-bey

We ought to obey God rather than men (Acts 5:29).

A. Many people obey their own desires or seek to please other people rather than God.

B. God's blessings are promised to those who keep his commandments and do those things that are pleasing in his sight (1 John 3:22).

III. T-rust

And the LORD shall help them, and deliver them . . . because they trust in him (Ps. 37:40).

A. In today's affluent society many are trusting in their possessions. They depend on money instead of God.

B. We must not trust in uncertain riches, but in the living God, "who giveth us richly all things to enjoy" (1 Tim. 6:17).

IV. A-ccept

Nevertheless not as I will, but as thou wilt (Matt. 26:39).

A. Christ surrendered his human will to his Father's divine will. He died on the cross willingly to atone for our sins.
B. Our will must be totally surrendered to God's will also. We must give him first place in our life (Matt. 6:33).

V. L-ove

And this commandment have we from him, That he who loveth God love his brother also (1 John 4:21).

A. God loved us so much he gave his only begotten Son that we might live through him (1 John 4:9). We must love God without reserve too.
B. Total surrender includes loving others. A smile, a kind word, a good deed, or a helping hand may verify our love (1 John 4:11).

25

"These Three"

And now abideth faith, hope, charity (love) these three . . . (1 Cor. 13:13).

Faith, hope, and love are necessities for Christians. We should strive to increase in these qualities.

I. Living Faith
Even so faith, if it hath not works, is dead, being alone (James 2:17).
  A. Faith is a must for Christians. God does his work in us through faith. We are saved, sanctified, and sustained by faith.
  B. To have a living faith we must also do God's work. Productive Christians should be happy and effective. They will receive their rewards in the life to come.
  C. We do God's work when we help the needy and oppressed, comfort the sick and lonely, and share Christ with the unsaved (James 2:14–17).

II. Lifting Hope
Why art thou cast down, O my soul? . . . hope thou in God (Ps. 42:5, 11).
  A. When the psalmist was discouraged, he called on God for help. He placed his hope in God and was lifted up from despair.
  B. In today's materialistic society many place their hopes in temporal pursuits or in the counsels of men. We must place our hope in God who never fails.
  C. We should say with the psalmist, "My help cometh from the Lord, which made heaven and earth" (Ps. 121:2).

III. Lasting Love
Yea, I have loved thee with an everlasting love (Jer. 31:3).
- A. Human love sometimes falters and fails. God's divine love never lets one down. God is love.
- B. God's love doesn't last for just a day, week, month, or year. His love endures forever. It is everlasting love.
- C. God loves through his people. His love enables us to assist the less fortunate, console those who are bereaved, and witness to the lost about Christ's redeeming blood (Eph. 5:2).

26

Victorious Living

But thanks be to God, which giveth us the victory through our Lord Jesus Christ (1 Cor. 15:57).

Christians can live victoriously. Victorious living here on earth fits one for the life to come.

I. Love the Lord
God so loved the world . . . (John 3:16).
   A. God so loved us that he gave his only Son to die on the cross as a sacrifice for sins. Christ loved and gave himself for us (Gal. 2:20).
   B. We must love God unreservedly. We must love our fellowmen also. Love never fails, for God is love. Love brings victory (Luke 10:27).

II. Live the Life
Strengthened with all might, according to his glorious power . . . (Col. 1:11).
   A. Many people make a good start. Then they begin to think they cannot live the Christian life. Soon they give up in despair.
   B. We cannot live the Christian life within our own power. However, we must never stop trying. Paul said, "I can do all things through Christ which strengtheneth me" (Phil. 4:13).

III. Lift the Load
That ye might walk worthy of the Lord . . . being fruitful in every good work . . . (Col. 1:10).
   A. Some Christians push down those who are already down. They do this to lift their own sagging ego.
   B. Our task is to lift the load of others. We must help the needy, lighten burdens, comfort the lonely, and love the unlovely (Col. 3:12).

IV. Lead the Lost

But speaking the truth in love, may grow up into him . . . (Eph. 4:15).

A. A smile, a kind word, a friendly response may be the means by which the Spirit-filled Christian can lead the lost to Christ. Ye shall be witnesses unto me (Acts 1:8).
B. Love the Lord; live the life; lift the load; and, lead the lost to Christ—and you will enjoy victorious living.

Will Answer in time — **27**

"W-A-I-T on the Lord"

Wait on the LORD: be of good courage, and he shall strengthen thine heart: wait, I say, on the LORD (Ps. 27:14).

Everyone is required to W-A-I-T occasionally. Here's how:

I. W-illingly

Wait on the Lord . . .

A. Many people are stubborn, set in their own ways. They fail to wait on the Lord because they want their own way rather than God's will.
B. We must realize that God's will is always best and "that in all things God works for the good of those who love him" (Rom. 8:28, NIV).

II. A-ctively

Be of good courage . . .

A. Some may believe that waiting on the Lord means doing nothing. They may become bored and negative when they have to wait.
B. It is said that the secret of patience is doing something else while one waits. We should seek to glorify God and be a blessing to others as Jesus did. He went about doing good (Acts 10:38).

III. I-ndefinitely

And he shall strengthen thine heart . . .

A. Many are ready to wait on the Lord but give up in despair if he doesn't answer at their appointed time. They forget that God's promise never fails. We must be willing to receive the answer when he chooses to send it.
B. We must never stop. We must keep on keeping on faithfully, assured that what he had promised, he was able also to perform (Rom. 4:21).

IV. T-rustingly
Wait, I say, on the Lord.
A. Today, millions are trusting in advanced educations, houses and lands, silver and gold, but few are trusting in the Lord.
B. People wait for the things they genuinely want. It is most important that we wait on the Lord—willingly, actively, indefinitely, and trustingly (Prov. 3:5).